Walking the Dog's Shadow
by
Deborah Brown

Winner, 2010 A. Poulin, Jr. Poetry Prize
Selected by Tony Hoagland

Walking the Dog's Shadow

Poems by

Deborah Brown

Foreword by Tony Hoagland

A. POULIN, JR. NEW POETS OF AMERICA SERIES, NO. 33

BOA Editions, Ltd. ❋ Rochester, NY ❋ 2011

Copyright © 2011 by Deborah Brown
Foreword copyright © 2011 by Tony Hoagland
All rights reserved

First Edition
11 12 13 14   7 6 5 4 3 2 1

For information about permission to reuse any material from this book please contact
The Permissions Company at www.permissionscompany.com or e-mail permdude@
eclipse.net.

Publications by BOA Editions, Ltd.—a not-for-profit corporation under section 501 (c)
(3) of the United States Internal Revenue Code—are made possible with funds from a
variety of sources, including public funds from the New York State Council on the Arts, a
state agency; the Literature Program of the National Endowment for the Arts; the County
of Monroe, NY; the Lannan Foundation for support of the Lannan Translations Selection
Series; the Sonia Raiziss Giop Charitable Foundation; the Mary S. Mulligan Charitable
Trust; the Rochester Area Community Foundation; the Arts & Cultural Council for
Greater Rochester; the Steeple-Jack Fund; the Ames-Amzalak Memorial Trust in memory
of Henry Ames, Semon Amzalak and Dan Amzalak; and contributions from many indi-
viduals nationwide. See Colophon on page 78 for special individual acknowledgments.

Cover Art: "Katsura Highland Park" by Richard Margolis
Cover Design: Daphne Morrissey
Interior Design and Composition: Richard Foerster
BOA Logo: Mirko

Library of Congress Cataloging-in-Publication Data

Brown, Deborah, 1948–
Walking the dog's shadow / Deborah Brown. — 1st ed.
    p. cm.
ISBN 978-1-934414-47-7
I. Title.
PS3602.R6944W35 2011
811'.6—dc22
                          2010029676

BOA Editions, Ltd.
250 North Goodman Street, Suite 306
Rochester, NY 14607
www.boaeditions.org
A. Poulin, Jr., Founder (1938–1996)

NATIONAL
ENDOWMENT
FOR THE ARTS
A great nation
deserves great art.

State of the Arts

NYSCA.

To George

Wild is not the same as free.
—Maxine Kumin

Contents

III. READ BETWEEN THE LINES

Foreword

Deborah Brown's poems remind me a little of the great Polish poet Szymborska. Both poets make thinking look easy. Overwhelmed by the world, unqualified to fix anything, Brown's speaker remains calmly capable of thought. "I'm writing to you from inside, / in the thick of it," she says. And also, "Bowling alone is no solution." And "In college I was sure I had a soul ... What was I thinking?" Did I mention the collaboration of wit and heart, which also characterizes Szymborska?

Witty, indeed, but such lines are rich with the sentiments of a grown-up person, one whose imagination has collided with experience and been repeatedly chastened. Compressed. The result is that Brown's speaker is qualified to give testimony about the wide world that bruises our delicate human fruits, the brain and heart. One of the great pleasures of reading a grown-up poet is that beneath each line is audible the many lines that have been written and erased before it—a mature sensibility is one that has been built up through layers and layers of trial and error, made out of smudge and scalds and the healed wounds of earlier versions of feeling. What is it that they say? "Tragedy plus time equals comedy?" Then to time add resilience, and a game attitude, and a cultivated flair for speech, and you might get poetry:

> When my friend said I had a Byzantine mind,
> I saw lofty minarets, intricate woven fabric. He
> thought tangled neurons, epistemic confusion,
> bits of plaque at war college devising an insurgency.
>
> ("Don't Ask")

"The broken symmetry is everywhere you look" ("Askew")—it sounds like a lament for disarray for the disintegrating postmodern world, and it is, but then again the brush with irregularity is part of every modern poet—Brown's poems teeter and spin, seemingly out of control. It's an intentional and unavoidable dizziness. In poetry, as in physics, centrifugal and centripetal are the forces that tug and pull against each other, always on the verge of flying apart. "Take the tiny pieces and see if you / can make a life from them" ("The Back of the Bike").

Brown is also a rhetorician, an argument-maker. In the poem "Reprise," for instance, our poet resurrects the antique question, "Which is better, Love or Fame?", and stays firmly on the side of fame, until the last turn. Is it a perverse enterprise to submit Love's existence to the care of reason? Even so, Brown's faultless logic finds its revelation:

> Better than a lover's heart, the immortality of a name.
> Love versus Fama, the goddess, with her long purple nails,
> her sweeping cloak, her memories of Caesar . . .
>
> Even better than love, fame, for as long as there is illness.
> I see that if I had discovered Cushing's disease,
> I could have named it for myself. . . .
>
> They're all forgotten, those heroes.
> How much do we know of Cushing, or care?
> . . . so back to love, the desire for love, the one
> that costs everything, that shocks you
> when someone else casts a shadow on the map
> of the earth for the first time larger than your own.

I could quote from this collection all day, since *Walking the Dog's Shadow* has plenty of wisdom, in its buoyant, adventurous modality. So let me just say, the poems here are exciting to read, teasing and pushy and serious and smart and full of heart. In Brown's poems, our tour guide's glasses (which are needed, because the eyes aren't what they used to be) have somehow been misplaced. First she locates them, then finds a silver thread, which she follows down the winding corridors and stairways, to the deep part of the poem, where it touches life. Brown's poems aren't just about a eureka; they taste of the whole journey. *Walking the Dog's Shadow* is a beautiful book, wise and sure of itself, fresh with wit and gravity, humane and true.

—Tony Hoagland

I.
DON'T ASK

Proof

In my closet, the tongues of shoes are amorous.
So it doesn't matter where you are, or who,
it should be possible for the moon to reach a long arm
around a shoulder, for the sand dunes at Cape Canaveral
to roll out like a 1940's dance floor. It is always possible
for one thing to touch another, isn't it?

It used to be possible for the hanging branches of the willow
to wiggle in the breeze with no idea of a neck bruised by a rope.
A world where association was pure. Where "duck" meant
a domesticated aquatic, not a sniper's bullet about to deafen
your ear. When did the innocent part of the country become one
with the rest of the violent world?

My friend Tom says, "Innocence was hung out to dry
in the Garden, remember?" It's an old story, I plead, it has to be
told again every year or so, I wasn't listening the first time. It's like
kissing—you have to discover it for yourself. But, back to the shoes in
    my closet
and back to the dirt patch where the willow and I

started out together, where Ruth Canfield bequeathed me
the earth smell of spring planting. So am I going to thank the adventurous
tongues of shoes, Ruth Canfield long dead, even the pine woods where
I made camp and combed trails with my fingers? Gratitude is so passé
in the era of bailouts and Benazir Bhutto, of racism's latest masquerade
in the flag. Proving it's always possible for one thing to touch another.

Small Sorrows

You can start anywhere,
you can start with the hummingbird
that quivers at the feeder, or with a moon
lost in the corner, or the stray dog who creeps
to my window and breathes. But not with
the Lebanese woman on TV who sobs as she
trudges back to her house of rubble.

How can I tell you my small sorrows?
In Slovenia, at the Nazi prison in Begunje,
you can see the last writing of two British
soldiers. On the stone of a shared cell, each
scraped the facts he pared himself down to:
name, address, parents, schools, date of enlistment,
rank, battalion, date and place taken prisoner, and
the date which became the year of death.

I didn't want to start there.
I don't want to end there. But no matter where I start,
or end, I will tell you—that if I could
touch you, I would become a hummingbird, a hidden,
shining center. And the dog—she would
press her small, strong back into my hip.

Don't Ask

When my friend said I had a Byzantine mind,
I saw lofty minarets, intricate woven fabric. He
thought tangled neurons, epistemic confusion,
bits of plaque at war college devising an insurgency.
It got more complicated the day six World War II vets
spoke after dinner at the Town Hall about their times
in Africa and Italy, the endless transport, the training
in the desert for war in the jungle. Their sergeants were cards,
the boys full of boyish pranks and short-sheets. No one was
scared, no foxholes filled with water, no buddies died.
"I just did what I was told, kept my head down," they all said.
They knew what could be said after dinner sixty-five years later,
stories scrubbed clean of blood and pain.

How do you know what you've left out of any story you tell?
My grandmother cooked, spoke a little English and had one story,
about her twin sisters, who also wore long black dresses,
who also crocheted quick birdlike stitches. One twin fled at night—
she despised family life, all those births and deaths.
My grandmother savored the moment after
the hook pulls the new stitch through the old, the moment
before it finds itself a place in the expanding fabric,
and if she spotted a stitch out of place, one that migrated
on its own from center to corner of the antimacassar, she knew
it had been sewn by the spirit of the sister who never was seen again.

The Shoe That Dropped

The shoe you threw out the window
   tumbled toe over heel, heel over toe,
     down the fire escape, through the skylight

onto sliced tomatoes, splattering
   olive oil all over the TV, fax and calendar
     and the postcard you'd sent

of a double-decker red bus when
   an IRA bomb in the Catenham Pub
     had just blown seventy men and women to bits,

an event almost as commonplace
   as ailanthus creeping between charred bricks
     and mortar, crumbled and helpless.

But now the dust, another cloud
   of our unknowing, churns over
     the heads of cops and tourists,

because our souls evolved like this,
   from friction and disintegration
     from a leftover whiff of smoke.

Thick and Thin

I'm writing to you from inside,
in the thick of it, knowing you're well
out of it. The neighbors and the relatives,
a small girl in a red coat who is someone's niece,
all slide on the ice, looking left and right.
A lot of people can't stop doing what they're doing,
smoking, drinking, looking at porn.
One guy I know can't stop writing drafts of hate mail.
He sends the letters to his friends to proofread.
Another can't stop blowing bull horns in his office.
The animals, too. Coyotes come for a late lunch,
or say they are going to. The masked owls
are forthright about their desires.
When night swoops down, a beak pecks
my cheek. The owl is everywhere.

In the thick of it, it's hard to know if you've
swept all the beach sand from the kitchen
or massaged that poor fellow's back. It's not
just the traffic or the appointment to clean your teeth,
it's really the way someone was crying the other day
about a dog she'd lost, and someone else yelling
at a man who'd married someone on cocaine,
and the latest cases of pancreatic cancer. I'll tell you
the nice bits: the Sunday bagel, an old Dylan song,
Susi's birthday party tomorrow, she's 50.
And the really nice bits, now and then, the memory
of a walk in the woods on a sunny trail and where
we lay down. Still, most of the time,
it's story after story. Always something happening here.
Some days I wish it would stop.

Walking the Dog's Shadow

It's best to walk a shadow till he pants,
to let him roam a bit under the hemlocks
while you ponder the shade of boulders.
It's best to let grief enter you like this,
alone with your own black dog,
a drag on anyone's leash
along the logging road to the lake,
past loggers' landings and a clear cut,
across the brook's collapsing plank bridge,
past the neighbor's garden shrouded in plastic,
past no trespassing signs, a dried up vernal pool,
crisscrossed by trunks of grieving oaks.
Every night, eager as a pup,
this shadow leads you into the woods
and shows you how well it heels
at your side, this old black dog of grief.

Empty Red

That Venus spins backwards is a surprise.
Why wasn't I told before? And the planet WASP17
travels in retrograde orbit—that's going east to west—
the opposite of its star. What with carrying wisps
of orchids and the lace gloves I wear in the garden,
I'm in a retrograde orbit myself, writing notes
in reverse the way Beethoven did in the final fugue
of the Hammerklavier. It's the way I've always moved
while most astronomical objects paid no mind.
What is worse than travel in reverse?
This year a plague assaulted the hemlock,
itself famously poisonous, and then
a pestilence developed that fed on the plague.
It's also true that parasitic flies transform fire ants
into zombies that wander. It's wandering that
frightens. It's cold as Mars, it's no orbit,
it's a nightmare that refuses to speak, a bright red,
not the color of a scarlet tanager, or even brick
or blood, it's an empty red that walks away,
silent, with no suggestion, no response.

Reprise

Better than a lover's heart, the immortality of a name.
Love versus Fama, the goddess, with her long purple nails,
her sweeping cloak, her memories of Caesar, Alexander,
the wolves on seven hills.

Even better than love, fame, for as long as there is illness.
I see that if I had discovered Cushing's disease,
I could have named it for myself.
It's hard to maintain desire, that's part of it.

But who first ate a grapefruit or tweezed a splinter
or waved across the pampas at someone else,
initiating the habit of the raised hand?
(If you don't wave two hands, there could still be a weapon.)

They're all forgotten, those heroes.
How much do we know of Cushing, or care?
What about Harvey, before whom our blood
traveled uncharted paths? Or so I was told
in seventh grade. I never wanted fame,
so back to love, the desire for love, the one
that costs everything, that shocks you
when someone else casts a shadow on the map
of the earth for the first time larger than your own.

The Stalled Bus

Because the night pulled down its shades,
because the voices of the past point with a shaking finger
as they collide with voices from the future, because the earth
insists on an ovoid shape, and the moon
plans to move off course. Because I have had to
erase and erase. Because there is a woman I know
standing in the rain in front of the bus station,
while the waiting room there on Union Street
fills with people and smoke, and every night now
a greasy-haired man stretches out on a bench
because the shelter closed at the end of March
and the nights are below freezing in April.

Because I am not Cassandra,
only someone afraid of myself and afraid of
the others who are like me but have power,
because a stalled bus is parked in front
of your house and mine and the houses
themselves have withered like drooping November sumac.
Because we may be here for a long time and because
the reptile mind has emerged again this spring
to shed one skin and grow another.

Askew

If there is nothing new under the sun,
then what is that half-lizard, half-tomato-
like creature crawling out of the rocks?
If the God particle is still missing, the mating
of two species would be new, like Charm and Top,
the newest of the quarks, lined up like Snow White's
dwarves: Up, Down, Strange and Bottom. Still without
the God particle . . . that could be why our symmetry
is broken. There are too many broken hearts, broken
legs, broken lives. On the other hand, how could there
be a whole and happy life when matter only barely
outweighs antimatter, when we have no idea when
antimatter might say enough's enough and take over
and turn us all into—nots?

                        The broken symmetry is
everywhere you look, from the moose that fell into
the bathtub of water the horses drink from
when they are not pursuing the apple tree around the paddock,
to the last car bomb in Mosul. We don't know who broke the symmetry,
and I don't want to point a finger as though I were Uncle Sam
in a poster. But it certainly explains the two sides of everyone's
face, the two halves of anyone's heart, why the coffee cup slides
to the edge, not the center, why I follow you to somewhere
in Peru even after I'm told you're not there, the way
antimatter isn't here, but it could have been.

Man Saves Dog's Life

Nothing is the same, now that blue paint darkens
the street. Swimming in the river is forbidden.
You can find better years. Blue paint?
What shade of blue? Midnight, navy?
A can of paint follows me home.
It whines for a little supper. I'm looking at the pine boards
in the wall. The knots are bookended, they seem friendly
to each other. Still, we are all under compulsion.

Under the calm umber shades of our nighttime talks,
I learned what to say when our father went off the reservation—
cashing bad checks in LA and renting a car to run over my brother.
He hit our best green trash can instead.
Trash all over the street—including the brownies
I'd made and the red nightie my mother bought.
In Massachusetts, the headline *Man Saves Dog's Life*. True.
The victim? A pug. The attacker: a Rottweiler combo. And the hero:
a man, 72. At home it was not *Leave It to Beaver* or *Father Knows Best*.
Father got worse until he stroked out just as I was putting
on my wedding dress. And the spring air blundered
and stopped, dead silent.

The Back of the Bike

In the beginning you believe in the life of poetry,
later you hop on the back reluctantly;
you burn your ankle on the exhaust
trying to read *Paradise Lost*.

Once the mind was a fertile valley where weeds blossomed.
The mind was open then.
It waxed and waned like the moon.

Listen to the weeds,
listen to the growing of the unwanted.
Who is listening to the sound of death,
the way it creeps into the joints?

Wasn't the mind once a fertile valley?
My aunt couldn't get out of bed because
a bone would break. That's how I feel,
but nothing x-rayable is broken.

Take the tiny pieces and see if you
can make a life from them, I mean
one you could love.
Jonah and the whale may be the real story:

who will swallow whom during the next flood.
No, that's Noah, who thought civil unions were a good idea.
Which story is the one that governs your life?
In the middle of the night the sky lowers towards me.

It has driven the moon away from home
and taken the shape it has always wanted.
It has a mind of its own.
The planets commiserate, they are the poetry of remorse.

On Alert

Why is the center of Mosul so close when the night's
darkness drizzles down on our hair and shoulders,
a rain cold enough to turn to ice?
The night sprinkles darkness over us.
It hides the lilacs stripping down for winter,
and the coyote pack that howls a crooked path
closer and closer to the house. The night hides
the leaves that abandon the trees, that swirl,
dust devils on the empty road. At night the forlorn
colors compose a chiaroscuro that hides your truths,
your lies, the bombed-out places we all know.
Why is the center of Mosul so close when the night's
darkness drizzles down on our hair and shoulders,
a rain cold enough to turn to ice?

Remember Achilles' shield that showed
a vineyard, a farm, a festival and a court,
the city at peace, the city at war, engraved by the god
of fire? None of this is easy. I can feel the darkness
coming closer, speaking the way it does,
murmuring the news we don't hear
in the absence of night, the absence
of a shield. What can I use to shelter from this darkness?
Don't say your arm, don't say any human body.
The night can see through and around you, there is
no hiding. What is the darkness but a presence that churns,
stirs the air, the leaves, puts on alert the ears of the red fox.

Narratively Speaking

Just yesterday Dean Young said
I could tell you about the blue-fingered giant
who wears blossoms behind his ears and cleans
clothes better than Ivory Snow. And that was
before the woodpile squeaked its regrets. He
lets me tell stories and not believe in

narrative sense or the moon-deserted sky.
He lets me finish the plum juice, swing on my swing,
and remember my last meal with Aunt Hannah—
moo shi and plum sauce, when she sneaked out
of the nursing home.

Narro, narrare, drifts overhead
like a Coors balloon—the first Latin verb I learned from
Miss Barnes in eighth grade. Did a bloated sidekick of fear
ring the chimes? Narratively, it's time for a turn here,
towards the self if possible, time to reveal something
about the child I was, abandoned in my crib, and how
later both of my dogs died of cancer and my sister
said I ruined her life.

It may be time to tell the story
of the pot-bellied pig who went door to door collecting
old *Watchtowers.* Today the clouds hang
low as the brim of a cap on backwards. There's more that's
backward around here. I myself face south often. Dean agrees
life is not always as easy as buying an ankle bracelet.

II.
LISTEN

Clue

When the woman next door totters
in with a blueberry pie and a crestfallen crust
and stays to apologize
for the color of her house, her marriage made in haste,
the children she bore in not enough pain—

I am all heart on a day like this,
willing to feed my heart to the juncos
on the railing, to the green pasture
where an old bay and an older chestnut
graze with yellowed nubs of teeth.

I have the soul of a shamed child,
but I am all heart on a day like this,
willing to throw all of my hats over the car roof,
to scrub clean the scribbling on the sidewalks,
even the lines that rhyme.

I am almost ready to say to the men who remove their belts
to strap a child, "I understand,
you must have been hurt yourself."
In short, I become a fool.
And this didn't happen in the spring,
or on a warm June night, an extra glass of wine.
It happened on an icy day in February,
when I finally had a clue about who you are,
who I am, and what we might be doing here.

Listen

The waning moon is sharp at both ends,
it hurts your heart coming and going.

Stars lie to each other, that's why they
flicker. We tell stories, try to love,

try to make sense and end up on a swing
kicking the air out from under ourselves.

From the centrifuge, news of other particles:
atoms, cars parked in a blizzard within earshot,

unreachable. The last story you sent me burned
the motherboard until it smoked. Language is a fire

extinguisher on the ropes of the familiar.
We sink into the circles of hell's dialect.

From the rooftop,
one of our stars shouts instructions.

The Trap

I remember the smells in Spanish Harlem, how
I wanted to eat and eat—fried eggs, tacos, sweets
at two a.m.—the night I heard the shot, the danger.

Once, on Mt. Sunapee,
a trap set for another animal closed
around my dog's neck, and my dog thrashed

while he had breath and went quiet
just as the trapper came down the trail
and unlocked him. The dog breathed again

and died years later of cancer. Last night,
in an old film, a train to Delhi stops where a cow
is tied to the tracks: Hindus and Muslims

warring on the eve of India's freedom,
while in the first-class car the British look on.
Today, in the same sharp air,

I remember how the dog looked
trapped, and how I watched, keyless.

On Not Knowing Your Father

It's dangerous not to know your father,
but it can also be dangerous if you do.
Oedipus is the first I know of, and that
ended as it began, with blindness.

But it's also dangerous not to know
how a lawnmower works. My friend,
a sociology teacher, lost two fingertips
reaching into his. Now he's studying the sociology
of maiming and body dysmorphic disorder.

I am trying to imagine the pain of a phantom
limb, but the pain I imagine is a phantom, too. Not
like the pain Whitman saw when he nursed
his young men. Outside the hospital was
a pile of amputated hands and stubs of legs
left to rot. It was the year before
Lister discovered that carbolic acid stops
infection in wounds. The soul went first,
tossed on the heap, then the heart. My hearing
is a phantom now. In college I was sure I had a soul
and told a despairing classmate about its bravery
and hope. What was I thinking?

My speech drove her outdoors to look at the trees
whose new leaves also failed to cheer her.
Nothing as tender as the line my finger traced
along your cheek that day, when I thought
memorizing its shape would save me.

The Scarlet Letter Law Struck Down in Massachusetts, Spring, 2003

No more scarlet letters, no more
Dimmesdale tripping over the rosebush
Hawthorne planted at the courthouse door.
No catching a thorn in his Puritan trousers,
nor making public his wish
to parent his daughter.

Remember how Hester,
a seamstress by trade, embroidered
colored threads around and around
the "A" she wore on her breast? Ruby
reds, emerald greens in a wild-hearted
design, until the "A" resembled
a lush, tropical garden where peacocks
fanned their tails in invitation,
where the scent of gardenia
hovered, where ripe grapes hung
within the hand's grasp and poppies
hinted at pleasures alien to the New World.

Such a celebration, Hester,
of that scarlet "A,"
of a love secret and defeated.
Compared to you, I am a garden
whose seeds have floated away
in spring rain, who's left
with spotty, yellowed growth.
Oh Hester, still hailed by today's news,
Oh Arthur, who wouldn't wish for you
that joyous sin in the forest?

Mamaloschen

Do you believe the way the grass
trusts its roots to loam? What do you trust this way?
Has the word "underling" lingered on your lips as it has
on mine, as in "I am an underling of the dean of this
college?" "Ling," in case you haven't heard, is an elongated
fish, as well as a morpheme that "serves as a pejorative
or diminutive suffix," so you will not be surprised when
this poem morphs into my mother's story of her trip
to London when she yelled "underling" at hotel employees,
often, she told us, proud of speaking up. I tried to think
no evil, to think of her parents in the Lowell knitting
mills, of the money sent to Vilna.

                That was the time when
all good men came to the aid of the party, when she
went to typing school instead of college. Now is also
the hour, though I for one will not wear black pumps
and gloves, or drink a highball or a whiskey sour. I say
it's time we pay attention, have some goals in common.
Bowling alone is no solution, though of course Nixon
preferred it to swimming, and I admit my balls fly down
the alley like a cornet's swoop of sound, but only when
I'm alone. I also glissando poetically, line for line, when
I emulate the best models in town as they soar on
the lingua franca, or the mamaloschen, words as real
as the cow's tongue that hung in the butcher's window
on the block where my mother lived as a child.

                A slice of cow's tongue has
those rough puckers you feel on a cat's tongue when it licks
your fingers. If I lie here through the night, the cat will come

out from under the car, or wherever she hides. She does not
share the best places with me, even when I need to hide from
my neighbor who "borrows" water from our well. I wonder,
how deep do I own the water? Or the land,
for that matter. Oh my sad mother! If only you had roamed
on Bond Street, and tossed out the memory of the butcher's window.

In Spite of Time

Listen: we make the word conspicuous
in bed time, harvest time, solar time, double time.
I've told you: Time's an invader who aches in us.

I'm not playing with words, as dangerous
as lying naked with you in the meantime.
But listen. Leaves fall, the wind sounds malicious.

In your galaxy, you say, time will not be so imperious.
Days will be ordered, the hour shrunk, stretched on a dime.
There, time is not an invader but celebrates with us.

We say next, lost, the nick of, time: it's ubiquitous,
it reminds us of last time, a time bomb, wartime, lifetime.
How could anyone, listening, become impervious?

It's a pastime to taunt you with passing time, hazardous
since in your wisdom, you're inclined to say I'm an unkind
pessimist. For you, Time's not an invader aching in us.

If it's up to you, we'll disappear from here without a fuss.
As a scientist, you'll write a formula, shift the paradigm.
But listen to me: words tell the oldest and deepest part of us.
Time's an invader, an intruder, who aches in us.

After the Sky

After the sky fell
into crumpled brown leaves and the hills
wandered close to where you stood,
after the everyday losses, after
the long hiatus between dreams,

I saw that the earth was up to its old tricks.
No way to put that sky
in its place or talk the hills home.

Then Eli handed me a white flower,
a weed from beside the road.
I thanked him and he handed me another
so his mother could see. We performed
our thanks and congratulations.
Johnny had written to Betty,
and Janey returned the call from Bill.

After all of that, the sky was still
in broken pieces and the hills still as free
as the wild horses of the Camargue.
No catching them, not even once this year.

Elegy for My Sister

On the river's western side, the water
is rough, white-peaked. Pines lean.
I stand at the stove, an iron ring over it,
where a pot and a fry pan hang—
two fierce and indifferent children
held by their wrists.

Her copper-colored urn is in my hands.

Weak light reaches some branches,
even now, in winter. Others wither,
then die, as she did, as though
the cancer was another dark winter.

Suppose the sky had opened before
her death, suppose I had forced a place
between leaf and leaf, until branches parted
and a delicate finger of sun touched each of us?

The tide of the mind is ruthless, too,
if a poem can find some pleasure in a death.

The Graviton

Your world, my world, depends
on a particle much smaller than
an electron that can't be seen
or measured or found anywhere
by any experiment. It's bad enough
not being able to find good fish and chips,
or true love, or an immigration policy
everyone agrees on. But the graviton
has to exist, since everything else exists,
more or less, so the argument goes.
For instance, the ducks at Cape Coral,
with thick red skin, scar tissue around
their eyes. Sleepless janitors, they peck
all night in debris, firemen in drifts of ash.
Because of the massless graviton, you dance
the *nuevo tango*, teeter under streetlights,
crawl out from under the bed any morning,
summer or winter, to rub your cat's belly.
Or you decide to read Heidegger
on the origins of a work of art until
you're waterboarding in anti-Semitism.
Only the infinite lifetime of the graviton
lets us saunter along and change the sheets.

String Theories

I say nothing

about how fast the light travels
        or of Einstein's problem catching up with it,
                or of Ludwig Boltzmann, who killed himself

when scientists mocked his belief
        in other dimensions. Today
                the strings of Boltzmann's theory

have stories to tell, they
        pulsate to anyone's rhythm.
                I hold you in ten dimensions,

wish you safe in all of them.
        I know space and time curl around strings
                that give rise to the gravity

which holds us here, the way the notes
        of Mozart's Requiem scrolled
                on his last staves. The invisible strings

in us spin themselves into specks of light,
        and two new forces one strong and one weak,
                draw us together. This is the complicated

shape of our time together, our past and present
        woven into a fragment of the sky.
                It is an elegy to you.

The Stone Wall

It's not when you are lying here alone,
when the green of the leaves seems the color of your grief,
it's not when the neighbor's dog gallops like a lost foal
toward the moon, it's not even when the seedlings
tell stories about the earth they're planted in.
It happens later. Then the story you've been telling
tells itself, is written on the ceiling in Braille, on your arm in tattoos,
in the crude chipping on granite in a family plot that gives a child's initials,
a husband's name and "wife of."
That's when you know too many stories are being told,
so many no one has listened for a long time.
So now it's time for you to start to listen
to the insects that clamor outside the screen waiting to be heard,
to the confused young deer that wandered from side to side in the road
while you watched from the car and waited for it to decide,
which it did as its spindly legs lengthened
slowly and strengthened into a leap over the stone wall.

Unleashed

I don't want to believe that genes
have us all on a leash, that math is a matter
of neurons, that fear lives in the amygdala
of mouse and man, that the genes of the woolly
mammoth led him straight to extinction.

Who wants to believe that everything's
encoded—revolutionary action, bungee jumping
over walls and into hearts, passions like
John Donne's or the disastrous life of
a Caravaggio? Let's agree to believe

it's possible to sniff along, nose in the grass
or up the telephone pole of delight, unleashed.
I want to believe we can shimmy right out
of that worn noose. You slip yours, I slip
mine, we're off to the park in a sheer

Neitzschean will-to-power triumph
over everyone's mixed-up set of instructions
for living, though not the ones for kissing
in the back seat, or for being the child who sits
in a puddle, arms up in the air, almost squalling,
not figuring someone's going to pick him up.

Last Things

One thing doesn't have to follow the next.
What a pretense that was,
white patterns drawn on the floorboards
at dancing school by a man in patent leather shoes,
though, I admit, as satisfying to me then
as a rose window at Ste. Chapelle
that breaks your heart even today.

Behind doors: sentences, pieces of the season
come apart, the tree left behind,
gifts, the ribbons tossed away, the family dinner.
It wasn't long after that I lost them both.
The halls grew longer as the night went on
and mice scuttled back to the cellar.
I stumbled to the room with blue curtains,
where you stayed when you were in town.

When lightning eclipsed the sky, we believed
we'd shine, not fry. We believe nothing has been
found in the closet or under the sheets, nothing
lies in the mottled streets, the sacrificial houses
we see around us, nothing.

Around us, the badinage of the city, trash,
old directions. We shook our heads like old folks
worried by ice underfoot, the spaces between stairs
large enough to fall through, doors
that lead to a pitched roof
and a certain gray around the edges of clouds.

III.
READ BETWEEN THE LINES

A Family Story

Like that mouse
who clung to the cabin wall
by its pale, delicate nails,
its shapely knuckles curved tight,
and then its tail flicking
side to side like a tongue over
its plump thumb of a body,
as if joining the argument,
clawing its way up, swaying
until, in the morning, the soft
collapsed body of the mouse,
stuck half in, half out of the wall,
as though he'd heard beckoning
noises from the field, as though
he'd tried to drive straight through
and batter his small way there.

Read Between the Lines

If I read between the lines
of my brother's spreadsheet
listing one hundred and thirty-six
worries, with a column for degree

of stress, if I read between the lines
of your letter from London
where you just missed the train
exploding in the Underground,

and if my friend Ella,
from a Romanian orphanage,
had not read blurs and weavings
in my palm, and if I read between

the lines on Jenny's arms
made by the print of a Cassatt painting—
ghosts of blues, outlines of a dress,
an apple, I might have asked when

I saw Freddie Klein' s mother,
her built-up shoe, the line of numbers
blue around her wrist. I wouldn't have
been told. Why live in New Hampshire

if not to keep secrets from children
who squint at numbers, stare at their palms,
trying to read the lines. Back then, we didn't
know the numbers tapped into our lifelines, too.

Brokenhearted

When my heart falls out of my pocket,
it cracks like an egg on the sidewalk.
When it stays at home, it aches
like an abscessed molar.
When my heart spins like blood
in a centrifuge, it is type A, AB, O,
a kaleidoscope of red glass,
read for its secrets. It cries louder
than squirrels playing roulette
in the bedroom walls.

It wishes for a dock, a tuppence,
a Marvel comic, a coin in the Trevi Fountain.
It limps along the Crawford Path, it can never
scale all the 4000 footers. It lingers
on a loading dock, watching
a French boy sweat over a tipping dolly.
My heart types messages in Sanskrit,
Arabic, Swinglish, and Esperanto,
Shaw's unused language, universal
as sweat and war. My heart has a mind

for words, not meaning. It stacks them
like dishes on a shelf, no air between,
a faint clack when one shifts at night.
They are dishes to be served, a stroganoff
or bouillabaisse. My heart angers the angels
but shrinks into sandwich wrap
when confronted by devils. It longs for civility,
seeks a Quaker, a nun, an engine that can,
it lives by the tracks, it runs by the tracks,
it tracks the ruin of nations, it leaves no tracks.

Isadora's Scarf

I am not living the life of the autistic boy next door
who can squint at any BlackBerry or VCR so that it
never sputters again. Nor the life of the black and white
stray cat who cries for company but hisses when any cat,
dog or human comes near. And not the life of Nour, the baby
with spina bifida, who lived in her grandmother's arms until
those with the power to save—two governments, many diplomats
and an air force—did, and flew her to Atlanta for surgery. And I am
not living the life of the toothless man with knife-blade cheekbones
who simpered at something moving on the wall of Sardi's Diner.

When I put my hands over my ears, I know I am
a wave about to break on the seaweed and gritty shore
of Biddeford Pool. When the music stops, jump
from chair to chair, pass your life to the person on the right.
Someone ends up with the lives of Saddam Hussein
and Slobodan Milošević. No wonder these men can believe
in their own innocence, despite witnesses and graves.
It's hard to know what crimes you've committed,
versus the ones you wanted to commit. I never believed
the soul has to live on until it gets it right.
My own lost life? I look for it on this town's narrow roads,
I wait for decision's scarf to catch and twist.

For the Cousins

Forgive me for wearing a wool jacket this morning,
for eating eggs and toast with plenty of jam,
for putting my feet up,
for reading this book of poems
in a house where no one will knock
with a warrant or a black boot.

And forgive me the luck of a grandfather,
a second son, who left Vilna circa 1910,
his name garbled by an immigration officer
into the nicely English Towshire.
And what about those cousins?

Forgive me, cousins, the words on NPR
of a fifteen year old Albanian girl began this poem.
She will kill herself soon—her rape shamed her family.
On the street, a doctor forbidden to practice turns tricks.
But what difference how long I make the list? Cousins,
I had forgotten you until your eyes ignited in the faces
of these others and your voices sorrowed in their throats.

The Night Is Balmy

In a chainsaw dispute,
Joe Kelly bit his brother-in-law's nose.
Jerry Courser dumped three cords
of wood on his neighbor's dog.
That sort of thing.
No one could hear the guns from
the last war, either, or the one
before that. You can hear noise,
a baby's scream on *Gray's Anatomy*.
I can hear a cat squeal at the door,
I almost heard the *ronde de jambe*
of a doe. But what about hearing
the sounds of guns? Are we dead,
blind, mummified? In the middle
of the night, the sky lowers towards me.
It has a mind of its own,
but no secrets from anyone listening.

The Figure in the Carpet

On the faded red medallion of the rug bought
by your grandfather a hundred years ago,
a dead mouse, who makes a sort of figure there,
centered as he is, almost perfectly. The figure

he makes is not the kind in which we understand
why the Marchioness has lied to a friend
about the marriage that brought madness
and such poverty to a branch of the family,

and not even the sort of Kandinsky red spot meant
to affect the soul, and not the sort of figure
the lilacs make mid-May against a background
of sumac. The figure is not the figure the oak joists

make at the ceiling's peak, or the figure
a solitary skater might make in ice and air.
When I pass the mouse and walk into the dark
of the kitchen, I see the figure is more like

the sad one the two of us made, at opposite ends
of the empty table, but that's not quite it.
It's the rug, woven in Persia by unknown fingers, woven as we are
though we don't know by whom or how or when.

Behind the Door

What is hidden behind the door?
       That's an easy one. A rocking chair, a bathrobe, a movie screen.
But what is behind the look
       you gave me when I left?
Ideas of symptoms weigh down my heart. Cells interpret their genes,
       communicate ruthlessly without us.

The days are getting warmer,
       soon the themes could be readable. My eyes close as if in prayer.
I read how the brain is structured
       to make us believe, or want to.

It's raining this December, when it should snow,
       another sign. Now is the time, but it is always the time.
Although the fingers grow thicker,
       perfect typing goes on from day to day.
Words gleam brighter and greener
       even as we get used to them. It's no good
thinking about tomorrow, and now it's back.

I remember my grandmother
       from the old country and her feather boa
when the dimness of the landscape shines in the window.
       While trees almost genuflect, a lost dog appears
in the pastures of the farm where we used to live.

Lake Massasecum, November, 2000

for my brother

On the lake road,
        frozen cottages, closed asters.
                The pebbled sky gossips,
answers itself, a voice in the distance
        out behind the barn, wild, buried.

Nostalgia.

It's not what you think,
        not a pining for the past
                and seeing only its best side,
not a yellow photographer's light.
        An image darkens, seen as if for the first time
                in its acetic bath. That kind of surprise catches us
in short pants and party dresses, leaving us sad,

possibly.

And then there's nostalgia for the mask on Halloween.
        Weren't you there with us? No, of course not,
                you were too young. And now we are too old
for costume parties, and where we ran on a summer evening
        as the sun sat on the cap of the ridge—a time,
                exaggerated in my mind to distract
from the chafing, the burning in my chest.

This afternoon

I will jog along the same path,
        and feel your absence a foot or so away
                from my shoulder and how you feel now

four hundred miles away.
    It wasn't that you liked to run, far from it.
        You wanted transport to another world,

that was all

and so did I, though the worlds we imagined
    were worlds apart, apples and oranges,
        vermilion and coca cola.

The Museum of Your Life

And this empty frame?
Whose picture should stand on this shelf,
one of a person you couldn't love
or someone abandoned to save yourself?
What would have happened,
had your world not been divided across the grain
into larger and smaller, kill and devour?

Portraits of people you feared hang on the right,
facing the ones you tried to intimidate.
Your father first, fist raised, face tight.
The husband you left looks the other way.
For each broken bond, the date
of separation, framed in a plastic card.
A corridor of friends you've lost track of,
a college roommate who left for Jakarta,
even your dog, that long-eared mutt, who died dodging traffic.

Magritte's Dog

You don't want to lose
the last glance you'll ever have

      of a moon milky and deep in the palm of the sky,
      and you don't want to lose

this afternoon of mist and rainbow,
though the shaken glass ball of this planet
swerves closer to its final ditch.

      You don't want to lose the last word
      Magritte's dog sings when he flies over the roof
      with the mourning doves.

You don't want to miss your own dog's last cries
before the silencing needle when her weight doubles
and you can barely raise her body up from the floor
to place her in the coffin you've cut and nailed,
while night falls and stars, clouds and sky lie broken.

      In Magritte, fronds of ferns sprout
      birds' beaks and trees tumble like clowns.

Your dog is buried beside the garden,
and it's Magritte's dog, not yours, who soars
over the housetop and the moon,
who flies backward as Magritte's dog can.

      You don't want to lose this chance
      to paste your hands to the dog's back,
      like an apple painted onto a man's hat,

and gather speed, and you don't want to lose
a last glance back at your garden. You don't want

to forget how this planet shakes—
a bone in a dog's mouth.

GPS System

So longing ends with death?
    I can't wait for that. Right now I want
        not to want. Not even the blossom.
I don't like the trying. I want it to happen like morning.
    The light reaches in the open window
        and there it is illuminating the white pillow slip,
            your hand, one side of your face.

I've developed a bad habit,
    like leaving a wallet in a different pocket every day,
        like forgetting to turn on the oven or to start the car,
like forgetting to wake up knowing it's a new day
    when it is a new day, and clouds hurry across
        the gray sky so it can change its tune.

When it is a new day, I will spend my capital,
    I will bike along the Southcoast,
        check out the battlefield in Hastings
where the language began, not far from the gray cliffs,
    the sheerness of them where they sheared off from the mainland.
        I cannot tie this together with the way fiddler crabs
calibrate their steps. Small crustaceans, they have homing skills,
    a mileage counter.

Do you know how many steps you have taken away and back?
    They do. Honeybees use the flow of the passing landscape,
        birds and sea turtles use the stars and the earth's magnetic field.
We are all somewhat magnetized, at least I am.
    And not by what I would wish.
        Once gone, whatever comes back?

Conjunctions Lead You Anywhere

Since the day I saw you on the end of the pier
when we walked back into a vast disturbed landscape,
although we agreed that
a conjunction can take you anywhere from
after the war right up until the armistice.

While we wait to see who coordinates the days,
the sun's rising and setting, we
fail to know we're caught between
the devil and the deep blue sea,
while we, dreamers of connection,

conjoin the ox and the bow,
eggs and bacon, the cow and the moon,
lies and death, since, astrologically,
a conjunction is a fusion. Nor is

"nor" extinct as a conjunction
even though "because" speaks to our reason,
even when our reason is wrong,
because we do not have enough time,
because I am not leaving as I planned and,
in order to have a peaceful night,
while the rushes sweep the riverbank,
and you said we might not have to leave
while the band played on.

A conjunction
offers the right conditions, if you look
the right places right in the eye,
then if you do not find them,

those sweet jewels of green grapes,
provided no one else is looking.

The Subjunctive

As in: what if Newton's apple were to "go sideways
or upwards" and "not constantly to the earth's centre"?

Or a prayer or wish: "Would that Caesar's ships had landed
elsewhere."

Or: Would that the opposable thumb were
the best thing that happened to us.

The man who wielded the hammer
to hit his wife might have dropped it before.

Would that Newton's theories
were wrong, and birds, planes and men,
answered to a magnetism stronger than earth's.

With age, lips and cheeks would round
up, bodies buried in the earth arise weightless,
matter-of-factly.

Earth might be empty underfoot,
a temporary depot, not
a resting place for mad orbiting life.

May the gods be pleased without landing here
on this clean earth, we might pray.

"Were this lecturer to carry on much longer, I might shoot."

"If it were now to die", said Othello, not anticipating the event,
"'twere now to be most happy."

Contrary to fact. We believe in them.

The sun traveled around the earth,
the fetid air of the Colosseum caused TB.

Would that the gods spoke.
Would that the hurricane struck elsewhere or nowhere.

Blackout

More and more poems wrest control of their future.
One deals only with stories about my father—
it loved the drama of a chair through a window,
a gun brandished at random.

Another prefers talk about my dogs, but balks
the moment the vet walks into the kitchen and kneels
at Jethro's pillow, a syringe in her hand.
This poem refuses to talk about the dead,
the wounded, the amputees, and it has a right,
like all of us, to look away from body bags.

No poem about a blackout soars: it is earthbound,
it studies a photo, a scrawny girl huddled under
a ripped sheet, sleeping in the street. When the power
failed last night and the computer screen blanked,
I remembered blackouts in London, the Blitz,
shared food and blankets in chilly cellars and now,
months without power or water in parts of Baghdad.
Camouflaged men patrol near the bank on the corner
where people deposited checks, paid the mortgage,
before the block was a pile of rocks and smoking metal.

After and Before

But it is surely always and only as we imagine?
—John Ashbery

Before I was endangered, a Hawaiian Honeycreeper,
say, I was another species. I may also have been
a blank sheet of newsprint used to wrap fish before
I came here in a dream. I hovered over cracks
before I heard the truck's transmission
and before I knew you, I expected someone else.

Before this war, there was another and another, so
before this melancholy, there was always melancholy,
so I knew no one was ever saved by someone else's hand,
or even by the art of Titian and Tintoretto, who plotted like
ordinary men, no better. Before it was easy to imagine blueberries
clustered thicker than stars, not touched by birds, rows of bushes
sloping as far as we could see, under a gold sun
that warmed our fingers. We dropped berries into plastic pails.

Before it was easy to imagine that kind of companionable delight,
how heavy the bucket began to feel, full after an hour,
the rope scratchy at the neck, before the weight of those berries
became heavier than the weight of anything else sweet, tangible, mortal.
That was before I imagined other mornings, each with its own weight,
before I understood how I imagined after and before.

The Chicken Soup

My husband made me
buy a road bike.
My niece talked me
into the alpaca skirt.
No one made me
adopt the cat
who sleeps on my pillow.
Fortunately, the cat
loves the skirt,
he thinks it's his mother.
But why have I turned
my life over to a cat?

My house is not gingerbread.
I'd rather discuss
the hospital as Kafka's castle,
your house as the mill on the floss,
the library as the tollgate,
the barn as opera house,
the opera house as animal farm,
the farm as the city bank,
and the city bank as the meat market
where I am the butcher
with a side of beef as a wall hanging
instead of that Picasso.

Where is the wall hanging going?
This is where the domestic imagery
so often flies into the chicken soup.
To the coal cellar.
When Bob was a boy,

he shoveled coal into the furnace.
What kind of domesticity is there anymore?
A TV breakfast, a shower or two, a space heater.

You can make your own list but
listen to mine anyway.
It's like yours and it's better
to beat drums in a circle or build sand castles
of denial and otherwise wax sentimental. Or.
The big Or. Or we can play with paints and words,
admire the kouroi and the Picasso,
the way we always did instead.

For Another Time

Afterward the swans lingered awhile
and the lilies swayed. The pond closed itself
up like a flower. Afterward they all knew.

The trash on the lawn blew away, leaves fluttered
monotonously. It wasn't a time for dancing, though
we had dressed for it.

It wasn't time for a party at all, not even for a dinner.
Better off going to the Tasty Shack for clams .
A man in shorts looked familiar, but we knew no one.

Afterward, the crowd looked as though
they had celebrated the end of something, maybe
a war. No Churchillian tones ringing on the air

this time. What did he say? He knew it would
be remembered by someone. Not by us.
Here the wind or a sound from below, like a furnace,

drowns out voices. Afterward was not unexpected,
but neither was it what we had hoped for.
Trills of lavender lace flickering were more like it.

Afterward, whether you'd been there or not,
there's a fragrance missing when you saunter
under a dripping awning. How do you know

when you enter another kingdom, if not by its scent?
Afterward, the atmosphere stuttered.
Parents, cousins, dogs I cared for were alive then

and never said a word about it. No one thought
it would come again, least of all me. I lagged behind
in the schoolroom, sang the doxology,

believed in the blessings that would flow.
And they have, in part.

Acknowledgments

Thank you to the editors of these publications in which poems appeared:

Alaska Quarterly Review: "For the Cousins";
Anthology of New England Poetry: "Clue";
Connotation Press: An Online Artifact: "Empty Red," "Narratively
    Speaking";
The Georgetown Review: "The Stalled Bus";
Hubbub: "The Scarlet Letter Law Struck Down in Massachusetts,
    Spring, 2003";
Hunger Mountain: "Mamaloschen";
Margie: "The Museum of Your Life";
The Mississippi Review: "Proof";
New Millennium Writing: "String Theories";
Poetry Miscellany: "Narratively Speaking," "Walking the Dog's Shadow";
Stand: "The Graviton," "My Head's in the Sand," "Reading Between the
    Lines."

"The Scarlet Letter Law Struck Down in Massachusetts," Kenneth O.
    Hanson Award, 2003.
"Clue," Editor's Choice, NE Poetry Society contest, 2007.

"For the Cousins" was reprinted in *The Other Side of Sorrow: Poets Speak Out
about Conflict, War and Peace*, ed. Pat Frisella and Cicely Buckley (Poetry
Society of New Hampshire, 2006).

The quotation in "The Subjunctive" is from *Memoirs of Sir Isaac Newton's
Life* by William Stukeley.

I would like to thank Richard Jackson and Maxine Kumin for their patient,
critical reading and rereading of these poems and Susan Thomas for being
my poetry buddy.

About the Author

Deborah Brown is an editor, with Maxine Kumin and Annie Finch, of *Lofty Dogmas: Poets on Poetics* (U of Arkansas Press, 2005) and a translator, with Richard Jackson and Susan Thomas, of *The Last Voyage: Selected Poems by Giovanni Pascoli* (Red Hen Press, 2010). Her poems have appeared in *Margie, Rattle, The Alaska Quarterly, Stand, The Mississippi Review*, and others. Brown teaches literature and writing at the University of New Hampshire–Manchester, where she won an award for Excellence in Teaching. She lives in Warner, New Hampshire, with her husband, George Brown, and four cats.

BOA Editions, Ltd.
The A. Poulin, Jr. New Poets of America Series

Colophon

Walking the Dog's Shadow, poems by Deborah Brown, is set in Bernhard Modern, a digital version of the font designed by the graphic artist Lucian Bernhard (1883–1972) and first cut by American Type Founders in 1937.

The publication of this book is made possible, in part, by the special support of the following individuals:

Anonymous
Jeanne Marie Beaumont
Jonathan Everitt
Pete & Bev French
Anne Germanacos
Jacquie & Andy Germanow
Janice N. Harrington & Robert Dale Parker
Robert D. Hursh
X. J. Kennedy
Rosemary & Lew Lloyd
John & Barbara Lovenheim
Boo Poulin
Deborah Ronnen & Sherman Levey
Steven O. Russell & Phyllis Rifkin-Russell
Vicki & Richard Schwartz
Ellen & David Wallack
Glenn & Helen William

Printed in the USA
CPSIA information can be obtained
at www.ICGtesting.com
JSHW082225140824
68134JS00015B/734

9 781934 414477